TIMELINE OF GEORGE GERSHWIN'S LIFE

1898 George Gershwin is born in Brooklyn.

1899 The Gershwin family moves to the Lower East Side of Manhattan.

1910 George begins piano lessons.

1913 George writes his first songs.

1914 George quits high school to work at a large music publishing company.

1918 George gets a new job as a songwriter!

1920 Famous singer Al Jolson records one of George's songs, *Swanee*. It becomes a huge hit!

1921 George is asked to write the music for New York shows. George's brother, Ira, begins writing the lyrics for George's music.

1923 George makes the first of many trips to Europe. He works on a musical play in London.

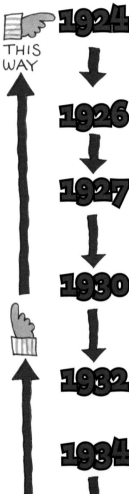

THIS WAY

UP HERE

1924 George Gershwin composes what will become his most famous orchestral piece, *Rhapsody in Blue*.

1926 While visiting London and then Paris, George gets the idea for *An American in Paris*.

1927 George tries painting with watercolors for the first time. Painting and art become an important part of his life.

1930 George and Ira go to Hollywood. They create music for many popular movies over the next few years.

1932 George vacations in Cuba and is inspired to write the exciting *Cuban Overture*.

1934 George has his own radio show. He begins work on *Porgy and Bess*. He travels to Folly Island, South Carolina.

1936 The Gershwins go back to Hollywood to work on more award-winning movies.

1937 George Gershwin becomes seriously ill. The world is shocked when he dies on July 11 at the age of 38.

GETTING TO KNOW
THE WORLD'S
GREATEST COMPOSERS

G E O R G E
GERSHWIN

WRITTEN AND ILLUSTRATED BY MIKE VENEZIA

CONSULTANTS
DONALD FREUND, PROFESSOR OF COMPOSITION, INDIANA UNIVERSITY SCHOOL OF MUSIC
AMELIA S. KAPLAN, M.A. IN COMPOSITION AND MUSCIOLOGY, THE UNIVERSITY OF CHICAGO

CHILDREN'S PRESS®

An Imprint of Scholastic Inc.

To the memory of my grandmother, Judy Strothers, who helped make music such an important part of my life.

Picture Acknowledgements
Music on the cover, Stock Montage, Inc.; 3, reproduced from the Collections of the Library of Congress, Music Division, George and Ira Gershwin Collection, reprinted with permission of Joanna T. Steichen; 4–5, Private Collection; 7, Culver Pictures, Inc.; 8, Los Angeles County Museum of Art; 16, Culver Pictures, Inc.; 17, Billy Rose Theatre Collection, The New York Public Library; 18, courtesy of the Ira and Leonore Gerswhin Trusts, used by permission; 19, courtesy of Mrs. Arthur Gershwin; 21, 24, Culver Pictures, Inc.; 26, ©Al Hirschfeld, drawing reproduced by special arrangement with Hirschfeld's exclusive representative, The Margo Feiden Galleries Ltd., New York; 27, ©1951 Turner Entertainment Co. All rights reserved; 28, courtesy of Marc Gershwin; 29, Billy Rose Theatre Collection, The New York Public Library; 30, Springer Bettmann; 31 (top), Culver Pictures, Inc.; 31 (bottom), 32, AP/Wide World Photos

Library of Congress Cataloging-in-Publication Data

Names: Venezia, Mike, author, illustrator.
Title: George Gershwin / written and illustrated by Mike Venezia.
Description: Revised edition. | New York : Children's Press, 2017. | Series: Getting to know the world's greatest composers
Identifiers: LCCN 2017022723| ISBN 9780531226599 (library binding) | ISBN 9780531230374 (pbk.)
Subjects: LCSH: Gershwin, George, 1898-1937--Juvenile literature. | Composers--United States--Biography--Juvenile literature.
Classification: LCC ML3930.G29 V46 2017 | DDC 780.92 [B] --dc23 LC record available at https://lccn.loc.gov/2017022723

George Gershwin, as photographed by Edward Steichen

George Gershwin was born in New York City in 1898. He became one of America's greatest composers. He is known for his beautiful, exciting concert pieces, as well as for the popular music he wrote for plays and movies.

George was one of the first composers to mix symphonic music with popular music of the day. He came up with a whole new American sound.

At the time when George was born, the United States didn't really have a serious classical music style of its own. Most American composers borrowed ideas from great European composers, like Beethoven, Bach, and Chopin.

George Gershwin, by David Siqueiros. 1936. Oil on canvas, 60 ³/₈ x 84 ½ inches. Private Collection.

There was a new kind of popular music, though, that was very American. It was called jazz. Jazz was invented by African American musicians, who used ideas from lots of different styles of music. They often combined work songs from slave times and religious folk songs (called spirituals) with exciting beats and rhythms. Two other styles of music that helped make up jazz were ragtime and blues. The musicians made up most of the music as they went along, and played the way they felt at the moment. Because of this, notes were never written down, and pieces never sounded exactly the same way twice.

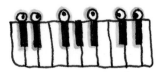

A jazz band in New York, 1919

Cliff Dwellers, a painting of a New York City neighborhood around 1900,
by George Wesley Bellows. Oil on canvas, 39 ½ x 41 ½ inches.
Los Angeles County Museum of Art, Los Angeles County Fund

When George was little, New York City was a pretty rough place to grow up in. Neighborhoods were crowded and there weren't many parks or playgrounds around, so kids had to play in the streets. George enjoyed playing street hockey and stickball. He learned to fight pretty well, too, and he was one of the best roller skaters around.

George didn't seem to have much of an interest in music until one day when he was seven or eight years old. George was roller-skating through a neighborhood in New York called Harlem. Harlem was filled with restaurants and clubs where jazz bands played. George never forgot the exciting, lively beat of the music.

He often roller-skated or hitched rides
back to Harlem, just so he could sit outside
the restaurants and clubs and listen.

A short time later, George heard some classical violin music being played from an open window. He loved the beautiful sound. The kids in George's neighborhood thought only nerds were interested in music.

George didn't care what anyone thought.
After that day, he decided he would learn
everything he could about music right away.

George started going to free concerts, where he enjoyed listening to classical music. He even experimented with making up his own songs on a friend's piano.

When George was twelve, a wonderful

thing happened. His parents bought a piano. It was really for George's older brother, Ira. Everyone in the family was very surprised when George started playing the piano as soon as he saw it.

Tin Pan Alley, 1914

George was lucky to find excellent piano teachers when he started taking lessons. By the time he was fifteen, he was good enough to get a job playing the piano at a company that wrote songs and printed sheet music. It was in an area of New York City called Tin Pan Alley. Singers and other show-business

Adele and Fred Astaire

people would stop by to listen to new songs for their acts. It was about the only way someone could hear a new song, since there weren't any radio broadcasts yet, and most people didn't have record players. George got to meet some famous people, like Fred Astaire and his sister, Adele. Sometimes George played his own songs for them.

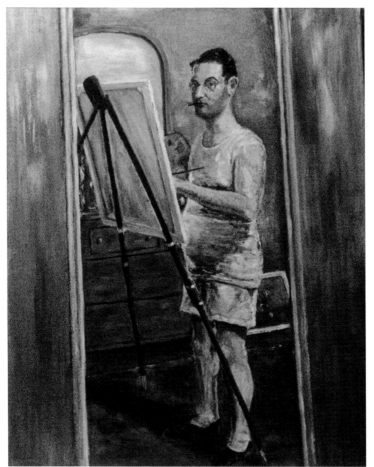

My Body,
by Ira Gershwin

George's songs were so lively and fun to listen to that it wasn't long before one of them became a big hit. It was called "Swanee." A famous singer of the day, Al Jolson, heard George play "Swanee" at a party and decided to sing it in his Broadway show. From then on, George found it easier to get jobs writing his own music, instead of just playing the music of other composers.

George sometimes asked his brother, Ira, to write words for his songs. Even though George and Ira were very different types of people, hardly anyone worked better together when it came to making music. George and Ira both enjoyed painting, too. Next to writing music, painting was George's favorite thing to do.

Self portrait of George Gershwin

GeORGE was becoming well known all over New York. He started getting invited to parties given by rich and famous people. Often, George was asked to play his music at the parties. He never seemed to mind, and sometimes played all night long!

One person who liked George's music a lot was a jazz bandleader named Paul Whiteman. Paul thought it was about time to prove that there was important music coming from America and being written by American composers. He decided to put on a serious concert. Paul asked George Gershwin to write a symphonic, jazz-style piece for his concert.

Paul Whiteman and his orchestra

George thought Paul Whiteman's idea
was great. This was his chance to show
how important American music could
be. George called his new musical piece
Rhapsody in Blue. He wanted his music
to have the sounds of modern America, so
everyone could enjoy it.

George wrote parts of *Rhapsody in Blue* while on a train trip. The noise of the steel wheels on the tracks and the train's clickety-clack rhythm gave George lots of ideas for his new music. He often heard music in the noise of machines and traffic and other big-city sounds.

Paul Whiteman's famous concert took place on February 12, 1924. People all over the country tuned in on their radios, and the concert hall was packed.

Besides George, Paul had invited several other popular American composers to play their newest music.

For the first hour or so, things didn't seem to go too well. People didn't find the music very new or interesting, and some of them were even getting bored! Then it was George's turn. George was at the piano, and Paul Whiteman led the orchestra.

Hardly anyone could believe their ears. *Rhapsody in Blue* began with a clarinet making a long, whooping, laughing kind of sound that had never been heard before. Next, the orchestra joined in, and finally, George Gershwin began playing.

When it was over, people couldn't stop clapping. They loved it.

A drawing of Ira and George
Gershwin by Al Hirschfeld

*R*hapsody in Blue made George Gershwin
famous all over the world. He went on to
write a lot more music for the theater and
movies, much of it with his brother Ira.

Leslie Caron and Gene Kelly in a scene
from the film *An American in Paris*

Many of George and Ira's songs became
hits, and are still popular today. George
continued to write symphonic music, too, like
Concerto in F and *An American in Paris*.

George Gershwin's favorite musical piece was his opera *Porgy and Bess*. An opera is like a play, except the actors sing instead of speak the words. *Porgy and Bess* was different from other operas, though. It was about poor African American fishermen who lived in a waterfront area of South Carolina called Catfish Row.

Program from a production
of *Porgy and Bess*

George Gershwin's sketch of his room
at Folly Beach, South Carolina

George traveled to South Carolina and
stayed near the people he was writing about,
so he could learn more about them and
make his music sound really authentic.

When *Porgy and Bess* first played in New York City, some people didn't like it. They weren't sure if it was a serious opera, or a play, or a musical comedy.

George was disappointed. He knew his opera was probably the best thing he had ever done.

A tense moment in
Porgy and Bess

George explained in a newspaper article that *Porgy and Bess* was a new kind of opera—a folk opera. It was about real, everyday people. The opera's music, too, was like the lives of real people. Some of the songs were fun and happy; others were serious or sad. Over the years, people began to understand *Porgy and Bess*. Today it is one of the world's most popular operas.

A scene from a 1943 production of
Porgy and Bess

George Gershwin (left) and his brother Ira (far right)

George Gershwin died in 1937. His music sounds as new and exciting today as it did when he first wrote it. Sometimes George used other things besides instruments to get just the right mood or sound. In *An American in Paris*, he used real taxi horns. In *Second Rhapsody*, he even used a fly swatter!

The best way to get to know Gershwin is to listen to his music. There are online radio stations where you can stream Gershwin's music for free.

LEARN MORE BY TAKING THE GERSHWIN QUIZ!

(ANSWERS ON THE NEXT PAGE.)

1. When George Gershwin was beginning his music career, he made hundreds of music rolls. What are music rolls?

   a A favorite bakery item among musicians.

   b A perforated paper roll that allows music to be played mechanically on a special self-playing piano called a player piano.

   c A platform with wheels that people use to roll heavy pianos from room to room.

2. **TRUE OR FALSE:**
Even after Gershwin became famous, he still wanted to learn more about music. He asked some top European composers if he could study with them, but they all refused!

3. George Gershwin was a good athlete. What were some of his favorite sports and games?

   a Tennis

   b Boxing

   c Video games

   d Ping-pong

   e Golf

4. George Gershwin and his brother, Ira, worked amazingly well together. Who were some other brother teams that worked together successfully?

   a The Wright brothers

   b The Smith brothers

   c The Coen brothers

   d The Everly brothers

   e All of the above

5. George Gershwin and other composers of his time sometimes used unusual "instruments" to get just the right rhythms and modern feeling to their music. What were some of those surprising "instruments"?

   a Airplane engines

   b Typewriters

   c Doorbells

   d A locomotive steam engine

   e All of the above

ANSWERS

1. b A music roll is a perforated paper roll used to operate a self-playing player piano. This mechanical method of listening to music was very popular during George Gershwin's time. Today it's still possible to buy music rolls and play them on a regular piano that's been converted to a player piano.

2. TRUE Famous European composers including Maurice Ravel, Arnold Schoenberg, and Igor Stravinsky refused to teach George Gershwin. They didn't want to influence him in any way that might interfere with his already creative and original American music style.

3. a, b, d and **e** As a young boy, George loved wrestling, roller skating, and playing stick ball, activities that were easy to do on the streets and sidewalks of New York City. When he grew up, George continued to enjoy all kinds of sports, and even took boxing lessons.

4. e: all of the above Throughout history there have been many successful brother teams who came up with great inventions, manufactured health products, and contributed to the film and entertainment industries.

5. e: all of the above Many composers during Gershwin's time used mechanical sounds to create music and exciting rhythms that expressed a feeling of modern times and everyday life.